# TECHNOLOGY IN ACTION

# BUILDING TECHNOLOGY

**Mark Lambert**

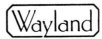

## Titles in this series

First published in 1991 by
Wayland (Publishers) Ltd
61 Western Road, Hove
East Sussex BN3 1JD, England

© Copyright 1991 Wayland (Publishers) Ltd

Editor: William Wharfe
Designed by: David Armitage

**British Library Cataloguing in Publication Data**
Lambert, Mark
    Building technology
    1. Buildings. Construction
    I. Title. II. Series
    690

ISBN 0-7502-0049-9

Typeset by Direct Image Photosetting Limited, Sussex, England
Printed in Italy by G. Canale & C.S.p.A., Turin
Bound in France by A.G.M.

**Front cover**  The latest in building technology: Los Angeles International Airport's Landmark Restaurant 'floats' above the tarmac.

# Contents

# 1 ▸ Building today

Buildings are so much a part of our everyday lives that we tend to take them for granted. However, as the world's population increases and old buildings fall into disrepair or become obsolete, there is a constant need for new buildings. You only need to look around your area and see how much building work is going on to appreciate how important the construction industry is today.

Every building has a purpose. We live in buildings that vary from single, detached houses to huge multi-storey blocks of flats. In addition to people's homes, we need schools, offices, factories and farm buildings. We also build roads and railways to make the transport of goods and people easier. Barriers, such as hills, mountains, valleys and rivers, mean that we often need to build bridges and tunnels.

Building design has altered greatly over the years. Here, in San Francisco, USA, modern skyscrapers rise above nineteenth-century houses.

In a sense, all the buildings that we live and work in have the same function. They provide protection from the elements – wind, rain, frost and snow. Every building must be strong enough for its particular purpose and most buildings are designed to last a long time. Ideally, a building should also be reasonably secure; intruders should not find it too easy to get inside.

Different types of building require different methods of construction. For example, a high-rise building must be much stronger than a two-storey house in order to prevent it from being blown over by the wind or collapsing under its own weight.

The cost of materials also determines how a building is constructed. For instance, making the walls of an ordinary house as secure as, say, a bank vault would make such a house very expensive.

The technology involved in building has advanced greatly during the twentieth century and improvements continue to be made. Some modern buildings may look similar to those built during previous centuries, but in fact their construction is very different. New materials have made it possible to make buildings stronger than before. New designs have also been made possible by the new materials. Many of today's buildings are quite unlike any built before.

**Above** Bridge- and house-building is combined in the *Ponte Vecchio* in Florence, Italy.

**Below** Modern technology can produce amazing structures – as in this plastics factory.

The first building materials were the natural materials people found around them. Wandering nomads lived in tents constructed of branches and animal skins. Then, as people settled down and began to farm, they learned how to use timbers – pieces of wood – to make more permanent constructions. Over the years they learned how to shape timber into beams and planks. Today, timber remains an important construction material. In regions where trees are plentiful, such as the USA, Canada and Scandinavia, houses are often built entirely of wood.

People also discovered that fine mud and clay could be fashioned into bricks, by pressing it into moulds. The moulded bricks were then tipped out and baked in the sun. Bricks of this kind were in use in the Middle East over 8,000 years ago. They could be reinforced to prevent cracking by mixing straw or animal hair with the clay. Sometime later, people in the Middle East discovered that if clay bricks were heated in a kiln, they became even harder. They baked, or fired, bricks at 1,000 °C, which is the temperature used to fire bricks today.

The fifteenth century 'Little Hall' at Lavenham in Suffolk, England, was constructed using a solid timber frame filled with brick and plaster.

Clay is a cheap, abundant material, and is ideal for making bricks. Here bricks are being made by hand with the help of a wooden mould, in Tanzania.

Bricks and stones became the most commonly used form of building material and remained so until the middle of the twentieth century. Bricks were all made by hand until 1825, when people started designing the first brick-making machines.

People also learned how to bind bricks and stones together in order to make a wall more solid. The Egyptians used gypsum (plaster of Paris), which is used today to make plaster and plasterboard. People then discovered that limestone when burned in a kiln forms quicklime, or calcium oxide. Greek and Roman builders used this mixed with sand and water to form a type of mortar. The same type of mortar was still widely used up until the late nineteenth century. Roman builders also mixed lime with volcanic ash and water, pouring the resulting mixture over aggregate (small stones of different sizes) to form a type of concrete.

Today, lime has been replaced by cement.

Portland cement, so-called because its colour is supposed to represent the colour of Portland stone, is made by heating limestone with a mixture of carefully selected clays. The mixture melts and fuses into a substance called clinker, which is then ground into a fine grey powder. Cement is mixed with sand to form mortar, or with sand and gravel to form concrete.

Large blocks can also be used for building. The first building blocks were cut from stone. Many beautiful old buildings, such as castles, cathedrals and even pyramids were built with stone blocks. However, for more humble buildings, stone blocks were too expensive. The first non-stone building blocks were produced during the 1930s. Known as breeze blocks, they were made of ashes mixed with cement. However, they were not as strong as bricks. Today, stronger concrete blocks are widely used for constructing walls. Some modern houses are built using small blocks of reconstituted stone.

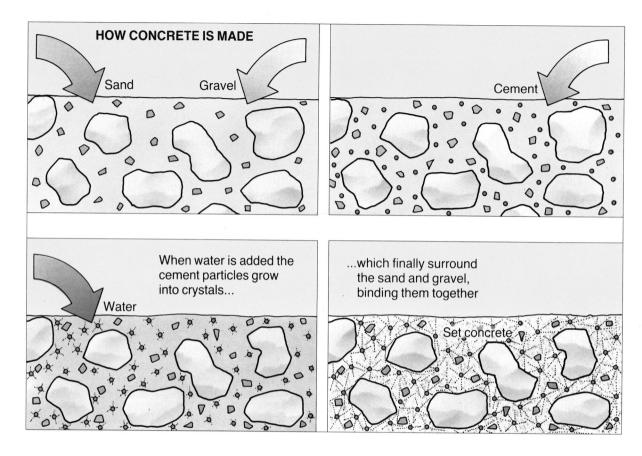

**HOW CONCRETE IS MADE**

Sand    Gravel

Cement

When water is added the cement particles grow into crystals...

Water

...which finally surround the sand and gravel, binding them together

Set concrete

Internal walls are usually constructed of lightweight insulation blocks. These are used to help stop heat escaping from the inside to the outside of a building. Modern insulation blocks are made of ash that has been ground up and mixed with sand, cement and water. Aluminium powder is added to the mixture and a chemical reaction produces small bubbles of hydrogen in the material as it sets. When it has become solid, the material is cut into blocks. The bubbles in the blocks make them good insulators.

Metals also play a major role in modern construction. Because they are stronger, steel beams, lintels and columns can be much longer than those made of timber. Steel bars and steel mesh are used to reinforce concrete. Fine steel mesh is used to produce a material known as ferrocement. Steel is also used to make pre-stressed concrete. Steel bars are held under tension along their length and then set in concrete. When the concrete has hardened, the tension is released. The steel bars contract, compressing and strengthening the concrete.

Other metals used in the building industry include aluminium and copper, which corrode less easily than steel. Pure aluminium is too soft for use in construction, but its strength can be increased by mixing it with small amounts of other metals to form alloys (metal mixtures). Aluminium alloys are used for making window frames and for cladding the outsides of buildings. Cladding can also be made of copper. Copper and brass (an alloy of copper and zinc) are extensively used in plumbing and electrical systems.

A range of other materials are also used in modern construction. Plastics are often used to protect a building against damp (see pages 15-17) and as light, waterproof window frames.

Other materials are used to insulate buildings; fibreglass and mineral wool are two examples. These materials trap air – which does not conduct heat easily – and so help to keep a building either warm or cool, depending which is needed.

Getting the design of a building right is very important, and designing buildings is therefore highly specialized work. A number of professional people, such as architects, design engineers, surveyors and structural engineers are involved. Detailed plans have to be drawn up in order to ensure that the builders know exactly how the building is to be constructed.

There are four important requirements of a well-designed building. First and foremost is function; the building must fulfil the purpose for which it is being built. What the building is to be used for will to a large extent determine the number, type and arrangement of the rooms inside. Thus a museum will be very different from a house, and an office block is designed differently to a block of flats.

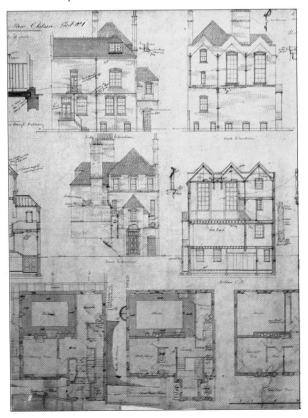

Design may also include such considerations as the cost of heating and lighting a building. Insulation is an important factor in cutting heating costs, and insulated walls, roofs and floors will form part of the design. Double-glazed windows will be necessary in an energy-saving house and glass panels may be used to trap the sun's heat. Clever design and placing of windows can also mean that the amount of expensive artificial lighting required in a building is kept to a minimum.

Increasingly, modern buildings are being designed with disabled people in mind. Ramps with handrails in addition to, or instead of, stairs, can be provided in order to give people in wheelchairs easy access into and around the inside of buildings. Signs in Braille can help blind people to find their way around. Where old buildings are not accessible to people in wheelchairs they can be adapted. A new home for a disabled person can be specially designed to suit his or her needs. In this way, today's building technology can be used by people with disabilities to help them live independently in the community.

The second requirement of good design is strength; the building must be strong enough to withstand all the forces to which it will be subjected. First, there are the vertical forces, created by the weight of the building and the additional loads it will have to carry when in use. These forces are transmitted downwards through the structure of the building to the ground on which it is built. Second, there are the horizontal forces to which the building will be subjected. These are caused by winds and earthquakes and vary considerably in different parts of the world.

Part of a design for a house. The drawings show the arrangement of the rooms from above (plans) and from the side (elevations).

In the UK for example, buildings will have to be able to withstand only the occasional storm force wind; earthquakes in the UK are rare and hardly noticeable. In other parts of the world, however, buildings may have to stand up to typhoons and severe earthquakes. In the city of San Francisco, USA, for example, there is a constant threat of earthquakes; buildings have to be designed to withstand them.

The third design requirement affects how the building looks. A building should, ideally, be pleasing to look at from the outside. It should blend in with, or in some way enhance, its surroundings, and its interior should provide a pleasant environment for the people who use it.

To some extent this aspect of the design depends upon the first two requirements: an attractive building is useless if it does not fulfil its purpose, or is dangerously unstable. However, even if the first two requirements are fully satisfied, there may be problems. A design that appeals to some people may not appeal to others. Often the most unusual designs cause considerable arguments.

**Above** Old buildings were usually not designed for disabled people. However, this stair lift makes it possible to get up steep, narrow stairs.

**Below** Earthquakes can cause buildings to collapse, like this high-rise in Mexico City in 1985.

In this unusual design of office building in Aylesbury, England, tinted glass panels on inwardly sloping walls are starkly contrasted with brick pillars.

Unusual designs often arise because architects and designers are striving to break away from traditional ideas and do something different. Modern materials can be used to create buildings with an ultra-modern, high-tech appearance. Homes of this type appeal to some people and many companies prefer to have their offices in buildings that help to give them a high-tech image. In recent years office buildings with exteriors largely made of steel and glass have become popular. There are, of course, problems with such designs. Buildings with large areas of glass tend to act like greenhouses with the sun heating up the air inside. Tinting the glass with a heat-reflective material helps to solve this problem.

The last factor affecting design is the cost of putting up a building. The cost of materials continues to rise, but the use of today's technology can help to reduce the number of workers involved and so reduce the amount spent on labour. It is, for example, much quicker and cheaper to construct a large, multi-storey building of steel beams, cladding panels (see glossary) and glass plates than it is to build a similar building of concrete, which would be much more labour-intensive. On the other hand, not all modern buildings are built cheaply. Where the appearance of a building is considered more important than the cost, designers sometimes include features that greatly increase the cost of construction.

On soft ground, long pillars, or piles, are sunk to provide a foundation. This machine is drilling the deep holes into which the piles will be placed.

The foundations of a building are the underground parts that hold the building firmly and prevent it from sinking into the ground. Without proper foundations a large, heavy building can become unstable and may well eventually collapse. The foundations of older buildings vary considerably. Most old houses are built on just a few layers of brick or stone.

In the Middle Ages French cathedral builders dug down to bedrock to ensure that their buildings would be well supported. In England, however, some cathedrals were built on wooden piles driven into the ground.

Modern foundations are generally made of concrete, sometimes reinforced with steel. The depth and strength of foundations varies according to the ground underneath and the weight of the proposed building. A modern two-storey house is usually built on a concrete foundation sunk about a metre into the ground. Where hard rock lies very close to the surface, a building can be constructed on a platform of concrete laid directly onto the rock. Sometimes bedrock can be found several metres below the surface. In such cases, foundations can be laid down to the rock. Rock is immensely strong and can support very tall buildings, which is why some of the world's tallest buildings are found in New York City, USA. The tallest New York building is the 415 m-high World Trade Centre; it is built on the rock that underlies New York's Manhattan Island.

In contrast, the tallest London building is the 183 m-high National Westminster Tower; as with all London buildings, its foundations are embedded in clay. It might well prove impossible to lay adequate foundations in clay for a building like the World Trade Centre.

Foundations can be laid in several different ways. The foundations of a house are normally begun by excavating a trench using a digging machine. The trench is then either completely filled with concrete or filled with a layer of concrete topped with concrete blocks.

Alternatively, long piles made either of steel or concrete reinforced with steel, can be driven into the ground. This technique is used for the foundations of very large buildings and where the ground is too soft to excavate (any trench dug in soft ground will fill in almost immediately). The pile-driving machine acts like a huge hammer, knocking the piles in a few centimetres with each blow. The piles are then cut off just above the ground and overlaid with a platform of concrete.

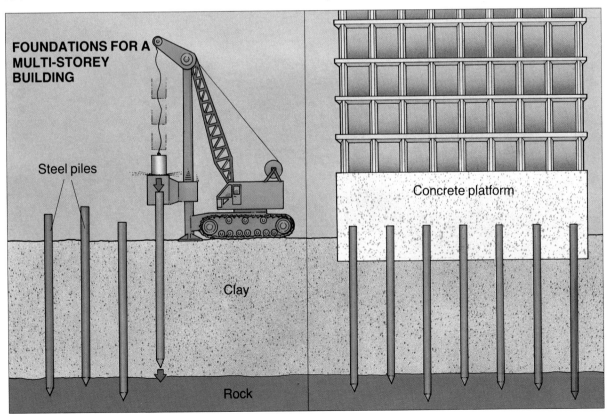

**FOUNDATIONS FOR A MULTI-STOREY BUILDING**

Steel piles

Clay

Rock

Concrete platform

Solidly-built walls have many advantages and people have been building such walls for thousands of years. They were used in structures that were intended to last a long time, such as temples, churches and monuments. Fortified structures such as castles and forts also needed strong walls. In many cases stone was used as a building material and the best builders carefully cut each stone to fit.

Working with stone was costly and time-consuming and most other buildings were built using cheaper materials, such as timber and bricks. Some builders did not trust brick walls to stay up by themselves. Instead they built a frame of timbers, which was then filled in with bricks. Today, bricks are generally used by themselves. Where timbers are included, it is for their appearance rather than their structural strength.

In this half-timbered house in Sussex, England, the main support is provided by the timbers. The bricks are used to fill up the spaces in between the timbers and to give a decorative effect.

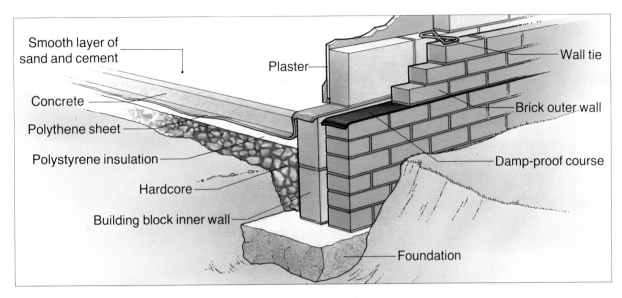

Smooth layer of
sand and cement

Plaster

Wall tie

Concrete

Polythene sheet

Brick outer wall

Polystyrene insulation

Damp-proof course

Hardcore

Building block inner wall

Foundation

**Above** It is very important that the walls and floor are built so that water cannot seep into the rest of the building. If water does seep in, and freezes in cold weather, it can cause cracks to form in the walls and floor.

**Right** Stone is an expensive building material, but is still used to build very solid walls. Building with stones of varying shape is a highly skilled craft.

Recently, however, people have started to build timber-frame houses once again. As before, the main structure of such a house is the frame of timbers. However, the frame is not filled in with bricks. It is given an inner covering of plaster board, an infill of insulating material and covered on the outside with waterproof bituminized building paper. An outer skin of bricks or other material is then built round the outside to provide a traditional finish and protection from the elements.

Older houses usually have solid walls. In the past, walls were normally constructed of two layers of brick or stone, sometimes with a layer of rubble in between. Some walls are built of a material known as cob, which is basically mud mixed with straw or animal hair to bind it together. To build a cob wall, the builder first used planks of wood, known as shuttering, to construct a narrow box. Semi-liquid mud was then poured into the box. When the mud had hardened, the shuttering was removed to expose a solid mud wall. The same technique is still used today to build solid concrete walls.

Modern houses have cavity walls, with a space, or cavity, between inner and outer walls.

Water, electricity and gas supplies are fitted as the walls and floor are built.

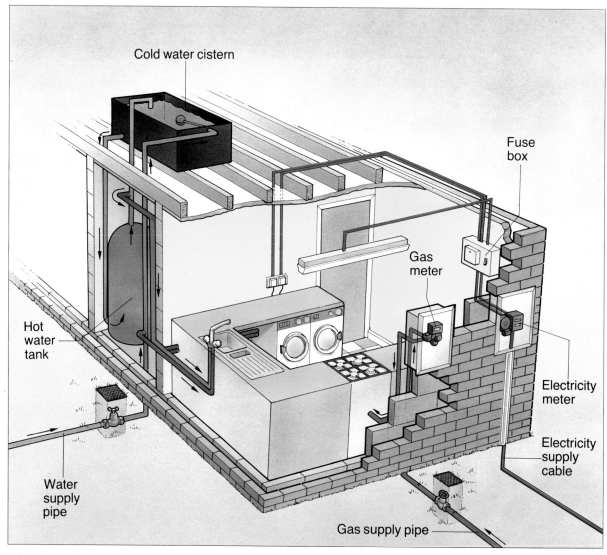

The cavity between the two walls prevents any damp that penetrates the outer wall of the house from reaching the inner one. The two walls are held together by wall ties, which are designed so that they do not allow water to reach the inner wall. The outer wall is generally built to look attractive and may be formed of brick, stone or reconstituted stone. A wall built of concrete blocks can be finished with a smooth layer of render (cement and sand mixed together with water) and then painted. The bricks or blocks are laid in layers, or courses (see diagram opposite). They are joined together with a mortar of sand and cement. Damp is prevented from rising up the wall by a plastic membrane, or damp-proof course, set in between the bricks or blocks just above ground level.

In some buildings prefabricated sections (sections of wall formed before being brought onto the building site) are used to build the walls. Modern prefabricated sections are normally cast in concrete, but other materials, such as cement-fibreglass mixtures can also be used.

The inner part of a cavity wall is usually built of insulation blocks, to help reduce heat loss, and finished on the inside with a layer of render and a topcoat of plaster. The cavity can be filled with an insulating material, which provides an additional barrier against heat loss.

Windows and doors are set into the walls as they are built. The top of each opening has to support the wall above. The support may be provided by an arch (see next chapter) or by a lintel. In the past, lintels were made of wood, steel-reinforced concrete or rolled steel. Today, builders generally use lintels made of steel formed into box sections.

The ground floor of a modern house often has a solid concrete base laid onto the ground beneath. A waterproof polythene membrane is set under the concrete and linked with the damp-proof course in the walls. This stops damp rising from the ground into the building. Above the concrete a layer of polystyrene insulation can be laid and the floor is finished off with a smooth layer, or screed, of sand and cement.

Alternatively, the floor can be constructed of

A cut-away section of a modern double-glazed window. The two layers of glass trap air between them. The trapped air acts as an insulator, keeping the heat in and the cold out.

wooden beams, called joists, set into the walls clear of the ground. This method is also used to construct the floors of any additional storeys. On top of the joists are laid a timber floor, either in the form of floor-boards or of larger sheets of chipboard. The joists are covered with plaster-board on the underside and the spaces between them in the loft space are filled with an insulating material to reduce heat loss through the roof.

Multi-storey buildings are put together using a variety of different methods. In some cases each floor is built as a unit on top of the floor beneath. Steel or reinforced concrete beams and columns support the weight of the floors above. In other cases a huge framework of steel is constructed first. The walls and floors are then built onto the steel framework. In another system tall steel columns are first erected.

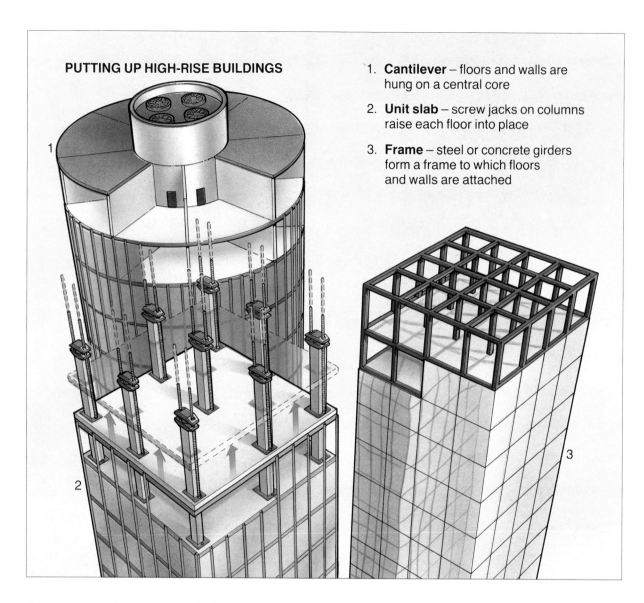

## PUTTING UP HIGH-RISE BUILDINGS

1. **Cantilever** – floors and walls are hung on a central core

2. **Unit slab** – screw jacks on columns raise each floor into place

3. **Frame** – steel or concrete girders form a frame to which floors and walls are attached

The required number of floors are then constructed at the bottom and lifted into place by jacks fixed to the tops of the columns. Alternatively, the floors may be supported by fewer, much larger columns; this provides more space inside the building. Yet another type of building is constructed around a single large column which acts as the central support for circular floors.

The 47-storey Hong Kong and Shanghai Bank in Hong Kong, which was completed in 1985, illustrates some of the construction techniques involved in today's large high-tech buildings. It was built using eight columns, each composed of four tubes. Each tube stands on a concrete pile that reaches 30 m down to the bedrock and 5 m into the rock itself. The floors of the building are suspended from five huge beams. The frames of these beams are visible from the outside and give the building a distinctive appearance. Most of the outer walls are composed of 13 mm-thick glass and the rest of the building is covered in aluminium cladding panels. These panels and other parts of the building were prefabricated, often thousands of kilometres from where the building now stands. Computer-aided design helped to make sure that everything fitted perfectly into place.

The Hong Kong and Shanghai Bank, Hong Kong. Unlike many modern high-rise buildings the main supporting frame can be seen on the outside.

An arch has two important features that have made it attractive to builders for thousands of years. First, it is a form of construction capable of spanning a large opening in situations where an ordinary beam might break under the strain. Second, an arch is pleasing to look at. Throughout history, building designers have found ways of using arches in their constructions, even in small openings that could just as easily have been spanned by ordinary beams.

A true arch is an opening spanned by a number of small wedge-shaped pieces of material that stay in position because they press against each other.

In an opening spanned by a beam, the weight of the material above presses down on the beam. This causes a lot of stress on the middle of the beam where there is no support from below. In an arch the load is transferred down the sides more efficiently. The load on the central wedge shape, known as the keystone, is transferred to its neighbours. These, in turn, pass their load onto their neighbours. In this way each block in an arch transfers the weight from above down each side of the arch.

If an arch is carrying only a small load, it can be free-standing. But an arch that carries a heavy load needs to be supported on both sides. Otherwise the upright parts tend to be pushed outwards. Arches are therefore often found set into walls or in very solid constructions, such as bridges. Arched buildings, such as cathedrals, often have special supports, or buttresses, built to hold up the main walls.

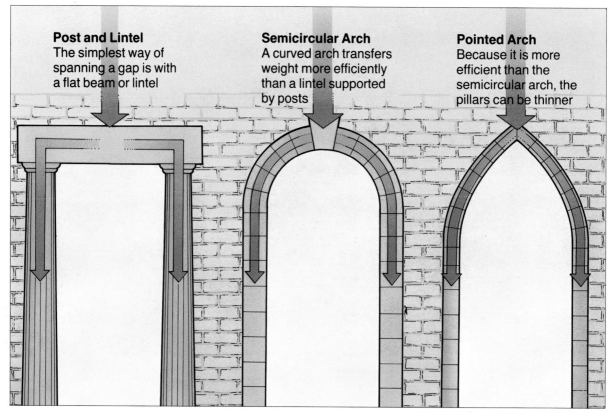

**Post and Lintel**
The simplest way of spanning a gap is with a flat beam or lintel

**Semicircular Arch**
A curved arch transfers weight more efficiently than a lintel supported by posts

**Pointed Arch**
Because it is more efficient than the semicircular arch, the pillars can be thinner

**Above** Here, in India, at Jaipur's City Palace, broad pointed arches are used to span a space leading into a courtyard.

The Gateway Arch, St Louis, USA, is made of stainless steel. It was designed by
Eero Saarinen and completed in 1965.

Arches were first used in Mesopotamia over 4,000 years ago. The Romans developed arch-building to a high level of technical complexity and throughout the Middle Ages European and Asian builders continued to develop different kinds of arch. From this period come the pointed lancet and Decorated arches, the curving ogee arch and the Perpendicular arch.

During the twentieth century, as strong concrete and steel beams have become available, arches in buildings have become less common. The most frequently used arch is the segmental arch formed over windows and doors in brick houses. In recent years, however, architects and building designers have started to include arches once again for their pleasing appearance. One of the world's most famous modern arches is the purely ornamental parabolic arch known as the Gateway Arch at St Louis, Missouri, USA.

Traditionally, buildings have steeply sloping roofs to allow rain-water to run off quickly. A roof on which puddles are allowed to form may be damaged by water or frost. Modern building technology, however, allows buildings to have much flatter roofs – which means that more of the space immediately under the roof can be used. These flatter roofs are made of materials that are less easily damaged by the elements, but even roofs that appear flat have a slight slope to provide drainage.

A roof needs a great deal of support. The roofs of early houses were supported by branches, and timber remains the most widely used material today. In a typical house the side walls are finished off with a beam called a wall-plate.

In an older house two or three triangular wooden frames, or trusses, rest on the wall plates and provide the main support for the roof. Horizontal beams, or purlins, rest on the trusses. The purlins support the sloping rafters, which rest on the wall-plates at the bottom and meet at a ridge-plate at the apex of the roof (see diagram). Battens fixed horizontally along the rafters support the outer roofing material, which may be made of slates or tiles.

The roofs of modern buildings are similar to those of the past, except that more trusses are now used. Because there are more of them they are smaller, and each one provides a rafter and a ceiling joist for the room below. No purlins are needed.

Many different roofing materials are used. Early houses were thatched with grass or reeds.

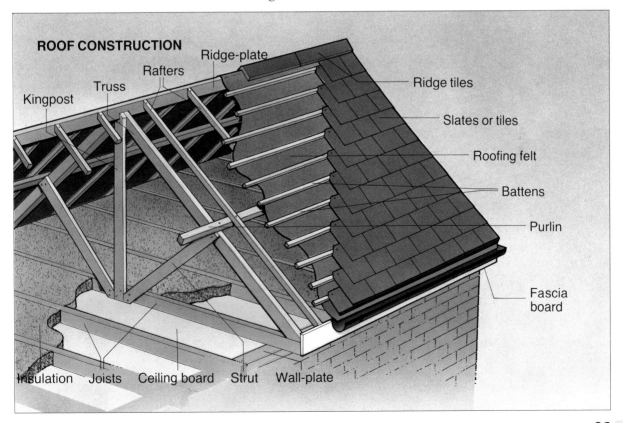

**ROOF CONSTRUCTION**

Ridge-plate · Rafters · Truss · Kingpost · Ridge tiles · Slates or tiles · Roofing felt · Battens · Purlin · Fascia board · Insulation · Joists · Ceiling board · Strut · Wall-plate

This form of roofing is still used in places. Slates and clay tiles are also traditional materials in many places. Modern tiles are generally made out of coloured concrete.

Flat roofs are usually covered with material impregnated with bitumen and reinforced with tiny chips of rock. This is fixed and sealed using hot bitumen. Some buildings are roofed with corrugated iron, which is popular because it is cheap. Recently, steel roofing sheets, coated to prevent them from rusting, have become available and these are now widely used for roofing industrial and farm buildings.

**Left** Covering a house with a thatch of reeds in Devon, England.

**Below** Finishing a roof with sheets of fire-resistant material that give a tile-like finish. The 'tiles' are being fixed with a staple gun that is powered by compressed air.

The first road-building began over 4,000 years ago as people dug drainage ditches along the sides of the trading routes between cities. Roman road-builders were the first to construct roads scientifically. Roman roads were built in layers, with a foundation at the bottom and a surface of paving stones at the top.

Before a modern road is constructed the route is carefully surveyed. Huge earth-moving machines level the ground, digging cuttings where the land is too high and building up embankments where it is too low.

**Right** Before a new stretch of motorway can be constructed, diggers and trucks may have to remove huge amounts of earth and rock. This is done so that there are not any sharp turns or steep hills.

Like a building, a road needs foundations. Without it, cracks, bumps and holes are soon caused by cars and heavy trucks. This is particularly important for main highways which are constantly in use. A road's foundation is generally formed of several layers of broken rock, each layer consisting of smaller pieces. Above this there may be a layer of concrete, sometimes reinforced with steel mesh. The foundation may also include a layer of bitumen to stop damp seeping up to the road surface.

The concrete is laid in slabs, with flexible joints in between to allow for expansion. Above the concrete a layer of dense tarmacadam, or tarmac (crushed stone mixed with bitumen) is laid. The surface of the road is usually made of two layers of rolled tarmacadam, which is often finished with a layer of asphalt (bitumen mixed with a fine aggregate, such as sand). The bitumen in the asphalt helps to prevent cars skidding. However, in some places surfaces are formed from concrete, which is more rigid than asphalt and spreads the load of vehicles more evenly over the foundation.

It is vital on a modern road that rain-water drains off quickly. The tyres of a car moving at high speed cannot grip a surface that is too wet. The road is therefore curved, or cambered, and given a surface covering of small stones. The curved surface allows the rain-water to flow off to drains at the sides of the road. The small stones create a rough surface which is easier for a car's tyres to grip.

Another hazard in wet weather is the spray thrown up by fast-moving vehicles. This spray can make it impossible for a driver to see ahead.

Laying down crushed rock for the foundation of a new road in Brazil. With a sound foundation, the road will be able to take heavy loads without sinking or cracking.

A road surface made of small pieces of stone embedded in asphalt. This helps
vehicle tyres to grip the road.

Recently, road technologists have developed a new surface coating in which a special kind of rubber-like plastic is mixed with the bitumen. This improves drainage and helps to reduce spray.

Plastic is also being used under the surface. Road-builders are now starting to include a layer of expanded polystyrene. This helps to absorb the vibrations caused by the traffic and thus prolongs the life of the road.

27

Mes Shkoder, an ancient arch bridge in Albania. The load at the top of the semicircular arch is transferred sideways to the river banks.

Bridges have been needed ever since people first started using roads. They are used to cross natural barriers such as streams, rivers, deep valleys and sometimes even stretches of sea. Railway construction also involves building many bridges, often where roads and railways intersect. Since the development of motorways and freeways, bridges have been used to allow roads to cross over other roads. Motorway intersections and flyovers are the bridges of the twentieth century.

There are basically three types of bridge: beam, arch and suspension. Beam bridges are the simplest type. Early beam bridges consisted of just a slab of stone or a few logs placed so as to provide a flat pathway over a stream. However, the weight on such a bridge acts downwards, through the middle and thus there is a limit to the span that can be achieved before the bridge breaks.

One way of making the spans longer is to strengthen the beams. In the past, beam bridges have been built using a framework of steel beams to form trusses. Modern beam bridges, such as those used to span motorways, are often made of concrete reinforced with steel. Alternatively, steel beams are used, in the form of box girders. These reduce the weight and cost of a bridge, while maintaining its strength. The first box-girder bridge was the Britannia railway bridge built by Robert Stephenson across the Menai Straits in North Wales in 1850. He used huge iron box girders and laid the railway tracks inside them.

Today, box girders designed for use on very large bridges are often streamlined to allow the wind to flow more freely past them. Some bridges have been destroyed by wind and so wind-resistance is a factor that bridge designers now take into account.

Beam bridges can be made longer by building supporting piers along their length. In North America, during the 1800s, bridge-builders constructed many bridges on a framework of wood. This truss construction was particularly useful for building railway bridges across deep valleys.

Another way of increasing the distance a bridge can span is to build a cantilever. In an ordinary beam bridge, the ends of the beam rest on a support at each end. In a cantilever a beam is pivoted, like a lever, on a single support. One end is firmly held down, giving the other end considerable supporting power. A cantilever bridge uses two such pivoted beams to hold up a third span suspended between them. The Forth railway bridge, completed in 1890, is one of the world's most impressive cantilever and suspended bridges – spanning 521 m.

Before the development of steel and concrete, beam bridges could only span short distances. Most bridges were built using one or more arches to support the load. The tendency of the load to push the piers outwards was usually overcome by building massive piers and using the banks of the river or valley as supports.

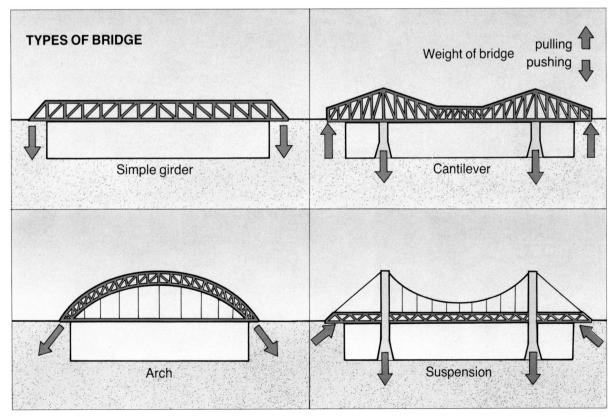

TYPES OF BRIDGE

Weight of bridge

pulling
pushing

Simple girder

Cantilever

Arch

Suspension

Sometimes a series of arches was built. In this type of construction each arch transfers the load to its neighbour until the bank is reached.

Early arch bridges were all built of stone and many of them were massive structures. More recently, people have constructed arch bridges of steel.

Among the most spectacular steel arch bridges are the 503 m-span Sydney Harbour bridge in Australia (completed in 1932) and the 518m-span New River Gorge bridge in West Virginia, USA (completed in 1977).

In an arch bridge the roadway is supported from below. In a cable-stayed or a suspension bridge, on the other hand, the roadway is on a deck supported from above using steel cables. A cable-stayed bridge has columns built of steel-reinforced concrete on top of the piers. A series of cables run from the top of each column to different points along the span. The extra support provided by the cables means that the deck can be made to span a greater gap. Early cable-stayed bridges had two sets of columns and cables, one on each side of the deck. A modern cable-stayed bridge, however, has one set of columns arranged along the centre of the bridge.

This beam bridge in Germany is being built of reinforced concrete. This way of building a bridge starts with a pier and works outwards.

The Golden Gate bridge rises above the morning mist. This suspension bridge spans 1280 m across the entrance to San Francisco harbour, USA.

Suspension bridges are used where very large spans are needed. This type of bridge also has columns built on its piers – one at each end of the gap being spanned. Two enormous cables run from anchorage points at each end of the bridge over the tops of the columns. The roadway is suspended from smaller cables that hang down from the two large cables. Much of the load is taken by the anchorage points and huge spans can be achieved. The world's longest bridge span is currently the 1410 m span of the suspension bridge over the Humber Estuary in England.

Tunnels are used to overcome a variety of physical barriers – hills, mountains, built-up areas and even seas. The method used for constructing tunnels varies according to their depth and, more importantly, the material through which they pass.

When building a tunnel close to the surface on land, a method known as 'cut and fill' can be used. First a cutting is dug down into the ground. Inside this a box or tubular construction is formed and earth is then replaced over the top. From 1863 onwards, most of the Metropolitan underground railway line in London was built using this method. Underwater tunnels can be built in a similar way. The tunnels that form part of the Chesapeake Bay bridge-tunnel system in the USA were constructed by lowering huge pipes into dredged channels and then pumping the water out of them.

Most tunnels are constructed deeper in the ground. In the past, the only way to dig such

**Below** The hydraulic jacks push the shield up against the tunnel face so that the tunnel does not collapse. Meanwhile the lining is put into place.

**Above** James Greathead's 1886 tunnelling shield, which used compressed air to stop the tunnel from collapsing as it was dug.

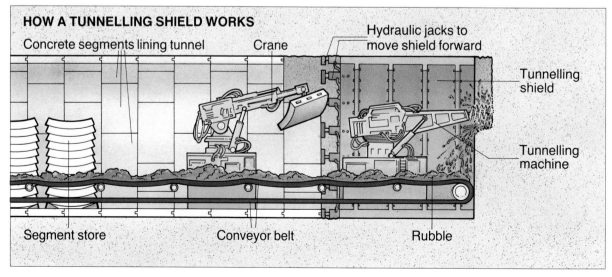

**HOW A TUNNELLING SHIELD WORKS**

Concrete segments lining tunnel · Crane · Hydraulic jacks to move shield forward · Tunnelling shield · Tunnelling machine · Segment store · Conveyor belt · Rubble

A modern drill and tunnelling shield at the end of a newly built tunnel. Unlike a full-face machine, the drill arm is flexible and is moved across the tunnel face.

tunnels was by hand, using pickaxes, hand-drills, rock saws and explosives. In about 1860 the French engineer Germain Sommeiller, while engaged on constructing the Mont Cénis tunnel through the Alps, devised an air-powered drill that enabled workers to tunnel more rapidly.

Tunnelling soft ground, like that found under rivers, was made possible in 1825 by the invention of the tunnelling shield by Marc Brunel. A tunnelling shield is a movable frame that supports the material surrounding the tunnel immediately behind the face (the point at which the tunnel is being dug). Brunel used a shield with a rectangular frame to build the Rotherhithe tunnel under the River Thames, completed in 1843. In 1874 James Greathead, another English engineer, improved Brunel's shield by making it circular. Later, while building tunnels for London's underground railway, he introduced the idea of filling the tunnel with compressed air to keep water from seeping in as the tunnel was being excavated.

A modern tunnelling shield is basically the same as Greathead's. It consists of a steel cylinder inside which the excavation process is carried out. Behind the shield a lining material is placed around the inside of the tunnel. This lining material may be constructed from concrete or metal sections, or a quick-setting form of concrete known as shotcrete may be sprayed on. As each section of lining is completed the shield is moved forward.

One of the huge full-face tunnelling machines used to dig the French end of the Channel Tunnel. The machine acts both as drill bit and tunnelling shield.

Where rock is very hard, tunnellers have to use explosives and machines. Modern machines include an electro-hydraulic hammer, or percussive drill, used for drilling the holes for explosives. Another machine, the Crac 200 fires a very high-pressure jet of water into a hole drilled in the rock to break it up; this is much safer than using explosives.

Most modern tunnels, however, are excavated by tunnelling machines, which have toothed cutting wheels that grind away the rock or soil.

In a full-face machine the cutting wheel covers the whole of the tunnel face, which is circular. In a partial-face machine, the cutting wheel is on the end of a long arm that is moved to and fro across the face. Excavated material is carried away from the face on a conveyor belt to trucks, which transport it to a tipping site.

When tunnelling soft ground, the tunnel face tends to collapse easily. This can be prevented by filling the whole tunnel with compressed air. However, compressed air causes problems for people working in the tunnel, and today the necessary pressure is limited to a small region close to the face. In one system, a quantity of special clay (bentonite) is held under pressure in a small chamber just behind the cutter. The bentonite mixes with the excavated material and is later separated for re-use. Another system, devised by Japanese tunnel engineers, uses a steel bulkhead behind the cutter. Air pressure on the tunnel-face side of the bulkhead builds up as more material is excavated.

One of the best known tunnel projects of the late twentieth century is the Channel Tunnel, being bored between Britain and France. Started in 1987 and due to be completed in 1993, this tunnel is being dug from both sides of the Channel, using eleven full-face tunnel-boring machines. The finished tunnel will actually be three tunnels running side by side. The two larger tunnels will carry electric railways, and between them there will be a smaller service tunnel. At intervals all three tunnels will be connected by service passages.

Altogether the Channel Tunnel (also known as the 'Chunnel') will be almost 50 km long and for 38 km it will lie between 25 and 100 m below the sea-bed. However, this will not be the world's longest tunnel. The Seikan tunnel, constructed under the Tsugara Strait in Japan, finished in 1985, runs for an impressive 54 km.

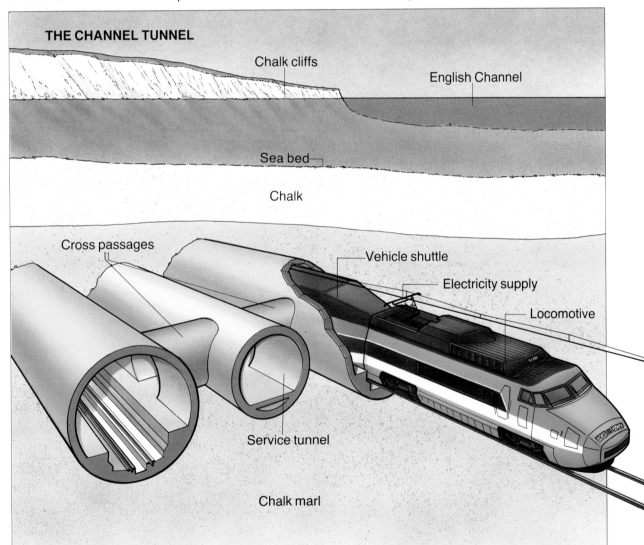

**THE CHANNEL TUNNEL**

Chalk cliffs

English Channel

Sea bed

Chalk

Cross passages

Vehicle shuttle

Electricity supply

Locomotive

Service tunnel

Chalk marl

# Dams

A dam is a construction used to hold back a quantity of water. Some dams are built to prevent flooding. Others are built to provide water for drinking, for irrigating farmland, or for hydro-electric schemes. The largest dams are the most massive of all constructions.

A dam is basically a large quantity of material placed in such a way that the waters of a river accumulate to form a large lake or reservoir behind it. Dams are constructed in various ways, depending on the amount of water to be held back, the geography of the surrounding land, and the cost.

The most massive type of dam is an embankment or gravity dam. A gravity dam is broadest at the base, where the pressure exerted by the water is greatest, and slopes up to a relatively narrow ridge along the top. A gravity dam may be constructed from thousands or millions of tonnes of soil and rock. The central core of such a dam is constructed from clay or concrete, which extends deep into the ground to prevent water seeping underneath.

Other gravity dams are built of concrete. In some cases such dams can be built leaving

**Above** Building the Itaipu Dam (on the border between Paraguay and Brazil). The main part of the dam, containing the hydroelectric power station, is on the left. On the right is the curved 'right-wing dam' which now guides excess water to a spillway.

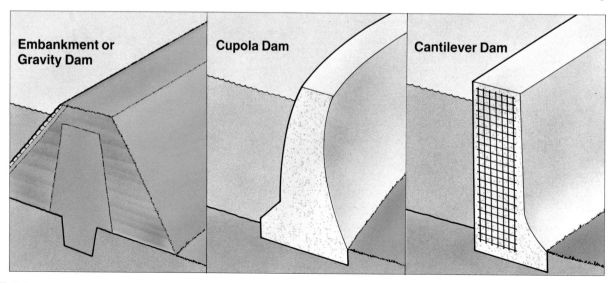

**Embankment or Gravity Dam**

**Cupola Dam**

**Cantilever Dam**

The Gordon Dam, Tasmania, is an arch dam. Dams like this hold back huge amounts of water which can be used for hydroelectric and irrigation schemes.

hollow spaces inside, which reduces the cost of construction considerably. The world's largest dam, the main part of the hydroelectric dam at Itaipu in South America, is a hollow concrete dam. This dam is nearly 8 km long, 180 m high and contains over 28 million tonnes of concrete.

Less bulky dams can generally be built more quickly, and may well be cheaper. Straight dams are sometimes built using buttresses for support.

Another alternative is a cantilever dam, which is reinforced with a web of steel bars (see diagram).

An arch dam is like any other arch (see page 20) in that the weight it supports (in this case, the weight of the water) is transferred to the sides of the valley in which it is built. A cupola, or overhung, dam works in a similar way, but in this case the dam is curved from top to bottom as well as from side to side.

**Above left** Some fifteenth-century buildings in Rouen, France, during renovation work

**Above right** The same buildings after renovation – ready for another few centuries of use

Some buildings last longer than others, but there comes a time in the life of any building when a decision has to be made about its future. Over the years some of the materials with which the building was constructed may have deteriorated. It may also be the case that the building's design may no longer be suited to modern use. For instance, a factory designed for a large number of people working on a production line may have to be completely renovated so that robots can be used.

Old houses, especially those built over 100 years ago, are generally prized for their appearance and historical value. Many are considered worth renovating and bringing up to modern standards of housing. Structural alterations may be necessary. Beams and other woodwork may need to be renewed, and walls may need rebuilding or at least repointing with new mortar between the bricks or stones. The walls may be injected with a special water-resistant material to prevent rising damp. Old plaster may

38

have to be stripped from the internal walls and replaced with new plaster. New electrical wiring may be necessary. All these things can and should be done in such a way that the building retains its original character.

It may be necessary to renew all the interior parts of a building, leaving only the original outside walls. Attractive old buildings that have to be altered to take modern office or factory equipment are often treated in this way. The building can be fitted with completely new floors, and if heavy equipment is to be installed timber beams can be replaced with steel ones.

Sometimes, an old building is in an inconvenient place; it may be in the way of a new development or road scheme. However, if the building is of sufficient historical or architectural interest, it may be possible to move it. Some buildings are dismantled piece by piece and then reassembled on a new site. In other cases it is possible to jack up a whole building on a steel or concrete base, fix wheels under the base and transport the building, intact, to a new site.

More usually, however, buildings are demolished in order to make way for new ones. Buildings that are of no particular importance, those that are structurally unsafe and others that have simply outlived their usefulness are treated in this way.

The method used to demolish a building depends on its size, the way in which it was constructed and on the value of the materials it contains. Useful materials, such as copper cable and lead pipes are generally removed first. A small building made with attractive bricks held together loosely by lime mortar may be worth taking down brick by brick. The bricks can be cleaned off and re-used.

Only the front façade of this old building in Melbourne, Australia, has been spared.
Behind the façade, new walls and floors will provide modern office space.

Digging machines, a crane and a wrecking ball are used to demolish a block of flats
that is no longer suitable for people to live in.

Alternatively, a brick-built building can be reduced to rubble by demolition workers equipped with hammers, crowbars and even pneumatic drills. The upper sections of tall buildings are sometimes removed in this way. The roof is removed first. Any steel beams are cut up using hydraulically-operated shears or a tool that produces a hot flame that melts metal, such as a thermic lance. When the structure has been reduced to a suitable height, the remainder can safely be demolished by machines such as a mechanical pulverizer, or a crane equipped with a wrecking ball – a large pear-shaped ball on the end of a chain – or an excavating machine equipped with a pusher arm instead of a digging bucket. Sometimes buildings are pulled down using steel cables.

A building on a level site that is reasonably far away from other buildings can be demolished by causing it to collapse deliberately, by weakening the supporting parts. One way of doing this is to subject steel supports to intense heat. A mixture of certain chemical compounds is packed around the bases of the steel columns and then ignited. The heat that is generated as the chemicals burn softens the steel, and the building collapses.

Alternatively, a building may be made to collapse by using explosives. Explosive charges are placed in carefully calculated positions around the base of the building, so that when they are detonated the building's supports disintegrate. A similar result can be obtained by using devices known as bursters. A gas-expansion burster is a cylinder filled with a chemical mixture that produces huge amounts of gas when ignited by an electrical spark. The gas expands rapidly and disintegrates the concrete around the cylinder. A hydraulic burster uses fluid pressure to achieve the same effect.

The most difficult buildings to demolish are those built using pre-stressed and post-stressed concrete beams. As the building is demolished the stresses contained within such beams may cause the building to break up too soon and, as the stresses are released, rubble may be sent flying in all directions. Great care has to be taken in order to demolish such buildings safely.

# Building for the future

As building technology advances, designers of buildings try to find new ways of using the materials that have become available. The use of new materials has therefore resulted in some interesting and unusual designs. However, the purpose of building is today broadly the same as it has been for centuries. We need buildings to live and work in, and a building that cannot be used for one of these purposes is of little use, no matter how innovative its design.

As the world's population increases, the demand for building will increase. The main decision that we will have to make is whether to build upwards or outwards. New office buildings, which are often built in areas that are already crowded, seem likely to rise higher.

The Financial Centre in Miami, Florida, USA, was built using modern materials.
The Metromover train in the foreground forms part of the overall construction.

However, there comes a point when you can build no higher; this is because the building materials and the ground underneath a skyscraper can only take so much weight before the whole thing collapses.

New housing seems to be going in a different direction. High-rise housing is generally unpopular today; few people like living at the top of a very tall building. Individual houses and, where necessary, low-rise blocks of no more than three or four storeys seem likely to be the most popular form of housing in the near future. However, space will be a limiting factor; eventually we will run out of land to build on.

Perhaps more buildings will be constructed underground. Offshore cities have been suggested as a solution.

In future, to reduce building costs, many houses may be system built; that is they will be assembled on site using prefabricated sections made of attractive, long-lasting materials. The design of such housing could be very flexible and it would be possible to lay out each individual house to suit the requirements of the people who will live in it. It should even be possible to build houses using movable wall panels, so that the layout of a house can be changed whenever the owners wish.

In Bombay in India, slums contrast sharply with neighbouring high-rise buildings, showing the need for more suitable and affordable housing.

There is no way of telling what houses may look like in the future. However, new design techniques and materials will make it easier to build houses with unusual shapes and even colours – like these in Auckland, New Zealand.

In the forseeable future it seems unlikely that there will be any major changes in the materials used for building. Concrete and steel will remain the most commonly used materials, together with timber, and clay bricks. Alloys of aluminium and other metals may be used increasingly, as will a number of plastics. As the world's oil reserves begin to run low and energy becomes increasingly expensive, energy-saving considerations will play an important part in the choice of construction materials for every building of the future.

# Glossary

**Asphalt** Tarry material formed as a residue when coal tar or crude oil (petroleum) is distilled. In some places 'rock asphalts' (natural mixtures of asphalt and rock) occur. They make useful road-surfacing materials.

**Beam** A long piece of squared timber or of metal, supported at both ends.

**Bedrock** The solid rock that lies underneath the earth's surface.

**Bitumen** Any of a range of sticky black materials that are obtained from the residue of distilled petroleum.

**Bituminize** To impregnate or cover something with bitumen.

**Cantilever** A support (usually a beam) fixed firmly at one end so that it can take a heavy load at the other end.

**Cement** A powder produced by pulverizing the clinker that is formed by heating a mixture of clays and limestone.

**Ceramic** A clay material that has been heated, or fired, in order to make it permanently hard and resistant to high temperatures.

**Cladding** The material used to cover the outside surface of a building.

**Cob** A building material consisting of clay and chopped straw.

**Column** An upright support or pillar.

**Concrete** A mixture of cement, sand, gravel and water.

**Damp-proof course (DPC)** A layer of material in a wall that prevents damp rising up the wall from the ground. A new house has a polythene membrane set into the wall just above ground level.

**Fibreglass** Glass drawn out into thin fibres and formed into a mat.

**Gypsum** A naturally occurring mineral composed of a form of calcium sulphate.

**Insulator** A material which does not conduct heat easily. Insulators can be used to keep heat inside a building, where it is needed.

**Joist** A timber or metal beam that directly supports a floor or ceiling.

**Lintel** A horizontal beam over a door or window.

**Membrane** A thin, flexible layer of material.

**Mineral wool** Rock wool. A fibrous material made by blowing steam through molten slag from a blast furnace.

**Mortar** The material used to separate and bind together the bricks, blocks or stones of a wall.

**Pier** A pillar that supports a heavy load. The main supporting pillars in a bridge are called piers.

**Plaster** Several forms of gypsum used to create a smooth finished surface on the inside walls of a building.

**Plasterboard** Plaster formed into a board by encasing it between two layers of heavy duty paper.

**Pointing** The even finish given to the outer, visible edge of the mortar between bricks or blocks in a wall.

**Purlin** A horizontal timber or steel beam that supports the rafters somewhere between the wall-plate (a timber that rests on the wall) and the ridge-plate of a roof. A purlin is itself supported by two or more walls and sometimes by one or more trusses.

**Rafter** A sloping timber that extends from the ridge of a roof down to the lower edge, or eave.

**Repointing** Removing old, decayed mortar and replacing it with new cement.

**Rising damp** Moisture rising up a wall from the ground below. See also damp-proof course.

**Screed** A layer of sand and cement used to give a concrete floor or roof a smooth finish.

**Tarmacadam** Bitumen mixed with small stones and rolled to form part of a road or runway.
**Tarred felt** Also known as bitumen felt. Any fibrous material, such as plant fibre, asbestos or fibreglass, impregnated with bitumen.

**Timber frame** A frame of timbers used as the main supporting structure in a building.
**Truss** A support consisting of a well-braced frame of timbers or steel beams.

# Further reading

Blackburn D and Holister G (Eds), *Encyclopedia of Modern Technology* (Hutchinson, 1987)
Clarke D, (Ed) *The How It Works Encyclopedia of How It's Built* (Marshall Cavendish, 1979)
Edom H, *How Things are Built* (Usborne, 1989)

Reader's Digest, *How Is It Done?* (Reader's Digest, 1990)
There are several relevant titles in the Wayland *Focus on Resources* series; for example: *Aluminium, Building Materials, Glass, Iron and Steel, Plastics, Timber.*

# Picture Acknowledgements

The artwork is by Nick Hawken (pages 8, 13, 15, 16, 18, 20, 23, 29, 32, 35, 36).

The publishers would like to thank the following for allowing their photographs to be reproduced in this book:
Barratt Homes 15 (bottom); Bridgeman Art Library 9; J. Allan Cash 6, 10 (top), 12, 22; Eye Ubiquitous 5 (top), 21, 28, 38 (right); Hutchison Picture Library 7, 26, 36 (top); David Kemp 43; Mark Lambert 17; London Transport Museum 32 (top), 33; Graham Rickard 14; Ronald Sheridan's Ancient Art and Architecture Collection 38 (left); Tony Stone Worldwide *cover*, 4, 5 (bottom), 19, 24 (bottom), 25, 27, 31, 40, 41, 42; Tasmanian Hydro-Electric Authority 37; Topham Picture Library 10 (bottom), 24 (top), 34; Zefa Picture Library 11, 30, 39.

# Index